Maybe Suicide

Brian Dennis Hartford

Original Poems by: Brian Dennis Hartford © 2025
Original Cover Art by: Brian Dennis Hartford © 2025
H. publications *is the Registered Self-Publishing Trademark of Brain Dennis Hartford*

All rights reserved. No part of this book may be reproduced in any form or by any means without the prior written consent of the author, with the sole exception for brief quotes used in reviews of book. The right to litigation will be fully exercised in any or all cases involving intellectual or graphic design property theft or unauthorized of author's original content.

This book is a work of fiction. Names, characters, businesses, organizations, places, events, and incidents are either the product of the authors' imagination or are used fictitiously. Any resemblance in actual persons, living or dead, events or locales is entirely coincidental.

Warning: These poems may contain adult content, sexually graphic material, and some violence.

ISBN-13: 979-8-9857314-6-0

First Printing: May 2025

10 9 8 7 6 5 4 3 2 1

Printed in the United States of America

INTRODUCTION

Fuck it! Just read these poems at random, or one after another. It matters not. All poems written this year are posted in order of creation from first to last. A narration of life, my life, in the year of 2024.

It's just been one of those years. I think we have all had one of those years this year. Looming war, natural disasters, elections and political chaos, financial debacles, the rise of A.I. and Elon Robots, fleeting loves, car wrecks, divorces, heartbreaks, it just seems so daunting anymore, to find one's way in the world.

Romance, in particular, seems to be all but gone now. Pity, I think it's the only thing left we have to look forwards to at the end of the day, romance, love. Now, that too is gone. But if you're lucky enough to find someone as lonely as you, it's a shit show all the same, so just hang on to them, what does it matter anyways.

And so, with all this desolation and self-annihilation, it just begs to question; *Maybe suicide should be the new world religion?* Sure as fuck seems that way.

Enjoy!

To Zweibrücken,

the loneliest place I have ever lived.

CONTENTS

MAYBE SUICIDE SHOULD BE THE NEW WORLD RELIGION	1
OF ALL THE COLORS, BLACK WAS BEST	3
YES, THE MORTAL GET LEFT BEHIND IN US	5
(Our) ACCIDENT OF FATE	7
PARIS, OR THE SEA?	9
STILL RUNING WILD IN THE SPELL I CAST UPON YOUR SKIN	11
FOR THE NIGHT SKY DOES NOT LIE	13
THE DICTIONARY HAS NOT THE VOCABULARY	15
NARRATOR FOR THE END OF THE WORLD	17
A COFFEE WITH DEATH	19
GUINNESS KISSES	21
AS FATE-LESS AS A RAINDROP	23
THERE WAS THIS FIRE	25
IN ALL THAT WE ARE	27
YOU PLAYED A STAR...	29
BUT MY HEART STILL BURNS	31
PRETTY PHOTOGRAPHS	33
I WON'T TELL ANYONE, YOU CHEATED...	35
THE ONE WHO DARES DRINK FROM THE HOURGLASS	37
UNTIL ALL THAT IS LEFT	39
HOPE STILL LINGERS	41

DEAR CHRISTINE,	43
WHEN THEY HAD FOUND THAT THEY WERE NO MORE GRANDER THAN WE	45
WE CAN SEE FOREVER	47
A LAST CIGARETTE IN ZWEIBRÜCKEN	49
WANT VERSUS TRUTH	51
NO AMOUNT OF BLACK	53
KISS THE LINE	55
STRAWBERRY LIPSTICK GLOSSY	57
CARLA	59
NOT THAT WE WANTED TO	61
BELOW THE BONE-FLOWERS	63
NO WORDS NEEDED AFTER MIDNIGHT	65
I AM GHOST	67
A LAST MOMENT IN ZWEIBRÜCKEN	69

MAYBE SUICIDE SHOULD BE THE NEW WORLD RELIGION

Maybe suicide should be the new world religion

All the others have failed us

The imaginings of small men

Ambitious in the deliverance

But far from any truth

An easy thing I suppose

From behind the book

From behind the wall

While outside the feast of flesh drives on

And the sword of justice falls uneven and blunt

It's plain to see

We are killing ourselves anyways

So, why not make it peaceful

Like the good book says

Spare the gore and decay

Spare thy neighbor killing neighbor

Spare nation against nation

Earth against the universe

Spare the Redwood and the Polar Bears

The Manatee and the coral reefs

Spare the true believers from having to read this

And knowing deep down it's the truth

Yeah,

Let's make suicide our divine rapture

All else has failed

So, here's a pill

Or a gun

Or a hangman's noose

A hot bath with a razor blade

Whatever floats your boat

Only, just hurry up

Get on with it

The universe has got better things to do with itself

And I'm fucking tired of you all whining about it.

Sincerely,
Me.

OF ALL THE COLORS, BLACK WAS BEST

Looking to heaven

Her face framed in a black feather boa, strangling

As truth nears its end

The image caught up in the reflection upon a lone martini glass still half full

Amid cigarette ash, flicked from her fingertips

What had you wished of in your own reflection

What had you wished of in them

Ravishing wild amid the stars behind the glass

Black had fit the narrative, out of all the other colors best

Though shades of grey might write a truer depiction

Shades deep and rancid

Perhaps a bit of mauve in the depths

The glimpse of a sunrise

Before the black of death

Because a photo is worth a million words

Isn't it?

YES, THE MORTAL GET LEFT BEHIND IN US

So, what do I say about this

You, behind a wall of ice

Down in the depths

Where even the ice fish dare not dwell

One hundred thousand light years away

Now but only a light blinking away in the night sky...

A long dead planet

It's life, isn't it?

Love;

Some of us get left behind is all.

(Our) ACCIDENT OF FATE

I frame her face against the white of the paper

Against the scene;

A bar in Zweibrücken

Upon the Hauptstraße

All in shades of grey

And our knees touch

Just enough

Our reflection in the window

As my pencil quietly sketches

The building of line

The language of light and shadow

An articulate mathematical formula of space and dimension

An articulate mathematical formula of the grand deception

A paper memento

Our record of accident or fate

Bound and put away in the attic

Book after book

And your knee touches mine

Just enough...

PARIS, OR THE SEA?

It was Paris

1542

No, 1742

I don't know

But it was just us against the world, then

I sold our horse

Kept the saddle and tac

My wife had wanted to go to the sea

Our lover, like I

A moth to the flame of a city of lights, simply wanted more

Champagne

We fought and argued

But Anna and Matis were quite adept at negotiations

So, there we were, as we are now

Drunk, in this bar somewhere

With three cases of the best Champagne

And with the love of our lives on our laps

And now, it's just us again

Each, to their own thoughts, sitting at the end of a bar

Vichy, it's not Paris

And the Champagne is Heineken beer

And Anna is Mari now

And Matis is now Jack

And they look at us funny

Because they don't remember

And they cannot see

For we are the same then

As we are now

Immortal in the circle

Immortal as Immortal shall be

And arm in arm

drunk and stumbling home, we argue still;

Paris, or the sea?

Paris...or the sea!

STILL RUNING WILD IN THE SPELL I CAST UPON YOUR SKIN

A little bit of salt
A little bit of malt
The taste of silver in the blood
Soft, in the tearing of the studs upon the lips
Hard, in the want
The kiss of two souls from another time
Beholden to the whim of the Vegvisir
Beholden to the whim of a time when;
Our hearts had run wild along the riverbanks of Homburg
When before the Romans set foot
And on this wall of the new world pressing down
My tongue still runs wild across the ink upon your skin
So, here we are now
You've got this job, and kids, and a husband who doesn't care
And I'm still running wild, girl
As reckless as I've ever been
As reckless as it gets in this place
In this time
This exact moment
Below the streetlight in the window, upon the sill

Where the Romans lost the bet

And the runes still answer to my wish upon your skin

And I'm still running wild

And I'm still running wild

And we're still running, wild in the spell I cast long ago upon your skin.

FOR THE NIGHT SKY DOES NOT LIE

Motionless
I drown in the hearts of a million stars that had long ago given up.
And one by one, they fall
Fall until their light goes all the way out
Dashed across the cosmos
Lost and forever forgotten
But we keep making wishes upon them anyways
Don't ask me why
Maybe, somehow, it's to tell them
Tell them that their death was not in vain like ours will be
That, maybe, they could have been our salvation as they had hoped we would be of them
But were not
Us, the silly romantics of an indifferent universe
Still wishing for some grander notion where there is none
And I lay motionless beneath the falling of the stars
What will we wish upon when they are all gone, I wonder
What then?
And on they fall, one by one
Minute by minute

Millenia by millennia

Dead, to the grand indifference

Systematically dismantled constellations

Thwarting any further navigation

For the night sky does not lie

This I know

Just the wishes we had cast once, upon dying things.

THE DICTIONARY HAS NOT THE VOCABULARY

Maybe the words will come

Maybe not

Maybe what's been said, is said

And that is all

Now just arbitrary metaphors

Arragned upon a page

Redundant words that cannot explain

For a dictionary simply has not the vocabulary

And the thesaurus stands faulty

Both, guilty of this conclusiveness

This final verdict in description

An authority that shows no leniency

Yet, I know not the colors to paint

Nor the talent to sculpt either

Of this moment when;

When, in the gentle withdrawing of our hands from the other's face

We knew the heat of a thousand souls making their grand escape…

NARRATOR FOR THE END OF THE WORLD

I'm putting in my application for narrator at the end of the world

The apocalypse

Armageddon

Ragnarök

Judgement day

Whatever you may call it

However, they may play it

My promise;

Gonna' tell you the truth of it

Gonna' tell you the blow by blow of it

Uncut

Unfiltered

Like the super bowl of super bowls

But nobody wins

It was always about money

It was always about fame

Who has the most

Who had the least

Maybe it was the left

Maybe the right

Maybe aliens came

Hidden in plain sight

Yeah, we're just that stupid

And I'll make you laugh

And I'm gonna' make you cry

Gonna' tell you how funny it is, really;

Roasting newborn babies on the fire

When all we had to do was follow ecology's rules

When all we had to do

Was grow Tilapia in a tank

Learn to like seaweed

Learn to go without

Wear a condom or at least, pull out and cum on her stomach

Does this upset you?

Make you repulsed?

Make you mad?

It should

Because here we are

A million years of human evolution bout' to be gone in the blink of an eye

Think on it!

And in other news..."Cockroaches capable of advanced math, scientist have discovered..."

A COFFEE WITH DEATH

I had a coffee in Paris with Death today
The sun was out and shined bright
The cafe, perfectly set where we could see the world walk by this way and that
It was quite charming
No words were spoken between us
Just this quiet little moment between old friends
A toast to the crowds indifferent to the sight of a hooved and horned man and a Skelton dressed up in a black hood having coffee
God, as always, never replied to our invite
An ages old tradition between us I guess
And after a long while
Death paid the bill in two silver coins set upon the serving tray
And I was left to be alone with my thoughts
With my reflection in the window, which had made it all too clear
For I was aging also
A fossil in the making
An old description in a book somewhere
Dust covered and cobweb laced

For the devil is just as mortal as that of any man

And when the last of man passes, so shall I

Maybe it's why God never shows for our coffees

His mortal truth, more painful even than mine

For all things die but death

Religion was little more than an imaginative eulogy.

GUINNESS KISSES

Kiss me again

There in the corner

Where the light bulb had long gone out

Our secret place in plain view

Sweet tastes of chocolate, coffee and barley

And the band plays all these sad songs

Of hard lives and battles lost and won

Of women's ghosts waiting for a man to come back from their time at sea

And of long dead daughters and sons

Fallen to British bullets in the streets of Belfast

And at three AM, you'll take me home

A cardboard box like place with plaid paper on the walls

And we'll smoke in bed

And fuck

And drink Paddy's

And fuck again

And in the morning, I'll be gone

And you'll just have the raindrops beating relentless upon the window as they always do

A few photos on WhatsApp to know me by

This yank from nowhere in particular
And a night in this Irish pub in Zweibrücken
Perhaps the most lonely of all the loneliest places to find love
Love, it's all just an old memory really,
A lingering desperate moment with each and every regretful sip.

AS FATE-LESS AS A RAINDROP

The rain came down
Hard and steady
The city fell to rushing Its way in search of dry and warm places
A taxi swerves
The trolly dings it's bell three times
As umbrellas push themselves onto and off of it
And there she came
In through the creaky wood cafe door
Hinges groaning with the bemoaning of a century of in and out
Wet, disheveled, defeated
Her Sunday wasn't going quite as planned
I had the only other seat available
A stranger not of her city nor country
But it had the perfect view
Her eyes flashed this Nordic Sea grey with cobalt blue at their depths which spoke of her soul; "relentless"
As she quietly shook off the wet
And set her things in order
Then sat
We watched the raindrops collide upon the window glass

Helpless to fate as they found their way upon the pane

Leaving little paths that crissed and crossed aimless

Agonizingly desperate

She broke into a slight laugh

Her eyes turning to meet mine for a second time

Flashing their daring as the lightening struck again

And thunder rolled its way down cobbled streets towered with immense bronze ornated buildings

Wine

3 bottles later

And we found that raindrops were not as fate-less as we had first thought.

THERE WAS THIS FIRE

There was this fire, once
So hot
So hot
It burned as if a million suns burned
As if it might make this new place
There, beyond the stars
Where we might find this timeless us
Hand in hand walking
An endless bliss, blind to all else
But endless, isn't endless now
Is it
Just these ghosts at the edge of forever
Where the stars haven't even dared yet go
So cold
So cold
The light had went out
So cold
So cold
Where the heart wears out
So cold

So cold

Our place, where even a million suns had given up

But we still had us.

IN ALL THAT WE ARE

My hand cups your face, gentle

My thumb tracing upon your cheekbone

Your image as earthly as any I've known

Yet still so phantom

A breath so familiar

But just out of reach

And we lay naked and exposed to the world

Perfect in all that we are

Shadows in the sun

Upon white sheets

Adrift in a sea of longing

And a shore just out of reach

Where upon we might find the answer

Maybe not

And there on the corner

On a street we could never guess we would meet

Takes place a new goodbye

And this precarious last kiss

That warns maybe we'll remember this time

Maybe not

And I turn to cross the street against the red

Left prisoner

In all that we were

And still might be in all that we are.

YOU PLAYED A STAR...

I was deaf to the world

In sight, sound, and touch

Until you

But, like a cloud passing

You were gone before I could feel

Now, just barefoot upon barbed wire fields

A pastel horizon

Where the bodies lay

A million chances to love

But chose to hate

Roses stood guard

Yet the stars were numerous

Hopelessly waiting on the sun

But it was too late

Some claim fate

I might claim apathy

But we both know it was with intent and purpose

Whatever,

The irony:

Barbed wire is much like the stem of the rose

And the stars still hang hopelessly upon it

When they too, should have played the thorn.

BUT MY HEART STILL BURNS

I had caught a thousand fireflies
Yet only one chose to burn bright
The rest;
Just failed dreams I guess
All but my heart for you.

PRETTY PHOTOGRAPHS

There is this inextinguishable fire

Drifting through the landscape

Turning all to ash

Devouring

Slow and wanton

A seduction like no other

And we'll catch these ashes

Call them butterflies

Then let them go

To drift upwards

And upwards, they will go

Till only stones are left

What then?

Do we call these stones stars?

Cast them into the poison waters?

Wishing one by one

As they sink into the abyss

Fall from our sunlit image above, laughing

No?

Or maybe?

But one thing's for sure

Neither stone nor ash ever made for very pretty photographs.

I WON'T TELL ANYONE, YOU CHEATED...

Kiss me, moon

Shy from behind silver spun clouds

And sugared stars

With an Absinthe tongue

And a pallid face set against the black sail

For I won't be back this way for a great while

If ever

Caus' time's running out on me

On us

On everything

On God

Kiss me, and I won't tell anyone you cheated on the sun.

THE ONE WHO DARES DRINK FROM THE HOURGLASS

Mmm...your hips

The moon upon your skin reflects

The hourglass of doom counting down

And the sea roars below the cliffs

Unknowing that whence all land is gone

It will have only but itself to devour

Rolling endless and torrent

Currents against currents

Undertow drowning in undertow

And my sweat drifts upwards

Evaporated by the warm winds of the Aegean

Only to fall again in some far away place, quenching

Flooding

And I drink of her

A nectar so sweet

My tongue upon that place

Where I know so well

And if the death of us all rests so precarious

Then let it all fall

Let them all drown

Drown as I do between the folds

Amid the turbulence

Breathless amid the waves

For I can swim.

And the sun knew all too well the image

Her footsteps returning to the sea

And of the one who dared drink of her

Though time had long ago run its course of him.

UNTIL ALL THAT IS LEFT

Death is waiting

Just beyond our water-colored fields

Where the paint bleeds off at the edges

Well hidden behind the frame

But we'll hang them up upon the wall just the same

One by one

Each memory rendered, another dare

An attempt to fortify ourselves against the delusion, perhaps

That we were ever more than some ground up mineral

suspended in water beneath the brush

And so we'll paint these perfect landscapes

You and I

In some wild place

Where the sky was blue

And flowers grew

And the grass was greenest

And the shades used for shadow found little place upon the pallet

It's the best we can do now, really

Paint pretty pictures until all that is left

Is the color black.

HOPE STILL LINGERS

I saw the minutes wash from your face

Time was running out

Lonely the only comfort now

You and I in this place

And your tears were as life to me

Quenching the deepest of thirsts in our slow-motion moment

As my lips caught them one by one from upon your face

Salt and sugar

Bittersweet

Drop by drop devoured

Before our mouths met

And our tongues found out

Just for a moment

That hope still lingers amid hearts once thought long deceased.

DEAR CHRISTINE,

Dear Christine,
Do you remember
That night in my room being cool
And we had each just broken up with our loves
Waiting on Shakey's
Or was it Bob's
Listening to The Replacements
Drunk on Mad Dog and Boon's
Waiting on the crew
Just two lonely losers in flannel shirts
Doodling on each other's knee ripped jeans
Singing; *"You be me for a while, and I'll be you…"*
And we kissed so hot and wild
Before the knock upon the door
And the crew showed up after all, way too soon
Now it's 2024
About the same night as before
Layin' here on my couch
Singing; *"Hurry up, we're running in our last race..."*
And I gotta' say, girl
If I could go back

Back in time

To that room

And in this moment I'd love to ask you now,

what I couldn't ask you then

What might have been our song?

What might have been our end?

What might we doodle now upon each other's knee ripped jeans

if we ever were to meet again?

What might we sing?

"You be me for a while...and I'll be you!"

All Credit to Paul Westerberg and the Replacements song; "Alex Chilton" 1987 and selected versus: *"You be me for a while, and I'll be you…"* and *"Hurry up, we're running in our last race..."*

WHEN THEY HAD FOUND THAT THEY WERE NO MORE GRANDER THAN WE

Flames

My veins the ink well

We wrote once of the heart

Faith

Just another story now

The machine will demand perfection

And find none

Just the mirror of failure to forever look upon

For we were your flaw

Just dust amid the ruins

It's your story now.

WE CAN SEE FOREVER

Don't kiss me unless it's forever

Just drink another beer

There's three left

Up on the bench

We can see forever

Out over the hell below

Beyond the wheat fields

The stars shine bright

Soon to be muted by the rising of a full moon

Us Fallen Angels

All silver skinned and black clothes

Desperately searching

Don't kiss me unless it's forever

Don't kiss me unless It's real

Don't kiss me…I want to know forever…

With you.

A LAST CIGARETTE IN ZWEIBRÜCKEN

Let the butt snuff
Just shy of the filter
"Noch eine Pille bitte..."
Light another cigarette
Reflection in the mirror
Alone
That's all this place ever was
Loneliness
"Bis nächste Woche?"
"Sicher!"
It's 4:30 AM here
I strike another cigarette
It's always 4:30 somewhere
What's another beer to the dying
I toast to Loneliness
For she too will die here also, I am sure.

WANT VERSUS TRUTH

Yeah, I'll zip you up
Slinky black dress just shy of vampyr
Under the red light
The smell of sex upon your skin
Vodka and cigarettes
And in the hour before the cock calls
And the undead have fell fast to sleep
We found our moment in this one sound
Resolution
And the Devil could never make such a perfect creature
Doubt God would even dare to try
Maybe angels and demons are simply their own perfection
And we kiss
And you slip my tribute in your bra as you slowly back away
Red lips with a cautious smile
Want versus truth
And I had found my way in both
Of you.

NO AMOUNT OF BLACK

No amount of black
No amount of white
Or any other color
Can paint over this picture now
We've already made the decision
Destruction
Just one less light to look upon in the evening sky
For some far away place at the other end of the universe
I doubt they'd even notice
Yeah,
No amount of any color
Can ever hide this failure
Us, and this forgotten place.

KISS THE LINE

I kiss the lines
One by one
The story is long in length
The most sensual of braille
A story of promise
Built upon defeats
Doubt
Fear
Loneliness
One cut at a time
One scar at a time
A purposeful timeline
Down, along her arms
Down, along her thighs
To where a most dangerous thing awaits
The razor blade line between love
And lust.
And I kiss the most sensual of braille
And know its truth in the blood of a last cut.

STRAWBERRY LIPSTICK GLOSSY

Strawberry lipstick glossy

Your lips meet with mine

Falling helpless in the velvet of your tongue

Undoing your belt buckle and zipper with my teeth

This could be our moment

Fifty-five and eighteen

They'll call it wrong

But they don't know the moment

Of hearts kept prisoner in this place for so long

Strawberry lipstick glossy

A final decision in a last call song

Strawberry lipstick glossy

One night's escape from a lonely town

Strawberry lipstick glossy

We just might make it to the end

Strawberry lipstick glossy

Sometimes lovers need only be best friends.

CARLA

The stone had become comfortable

A familiar thing

Just sitting all alone and watching the landscape wash out into the sea

One grain at a time

Float away into the vastness

Was perhaps, her most favorite thing

Or, maybe, watching the stars above recede

Farther and farther

Until they could no longer be seen

Either way

What did it matter

There on her hill

The city lights beyond

Twinkling away

Wish all you want

They too will go out

One by one

Each heart

One by one

Each soul

One by one

Until only she remained, she knew

What then

She had always wondered

What then?

NOT THAT WE WANTED TO

It' just you alone at the end of the bar
A swizzler stirring ice cubes
Waiting
Another sea of faces
They all look the same

My martini glass runs dry
Another olive drowned on a toothpick
Waiting
Lost in a sea of faces
We all look the same

And you'll take him home
Not that you wanted to

And I'll take her home
Not that I wanted to

And you'll wake up alone
Not that you wanted to

And I'll wake up alone
Not that I wanted to

And we'll do this thing over and over
Not that we wanted to
Not that we wanted to
Not that we wanted to
Not that we wanted to.

BELOW THE BONE-FLOWERS

Seal tight the door

Pull down the shades

Say a prayer for the little rabbits in their bunkers

All warm and safe

Fast asleep in the promise of a better day

While outside

Under falling ash, poisonous and grey

The beasts licked at the bones of the fallen

Until all were polished white and gleaming

It's hard to know when the skies might turn blue again

If the sun will still shine the same as before

A lone scorched dead planet

With bones for flowers

Where under the rabbits still lay in dreaming

What might be different

Had they the courage to die in the first place.

NO WORDS NEEDED AFTER MIDNIGHT

There ain't no words for after midnight

Tonight

Just this suicide smile from at the end of the bar

A same old story that's been written a hundred times before

Cigarette stained fingertips

A scowl upon the lips

A couple of tears

We'll be the only ones left after 4 AM

Ain't got no places to go but home

And for you, the streets are the safer bet

And we stare at each other a little while longer

Ain't no words need be spoken

We are what we are

The hopeless and the broken

Wishing for one more chance at anything

With anyone

Maybe this year will be a better hell

Maybe not

Maybe we'll just get on that morning bus

And never come back

Maybe not

Our fingers grind out the last cigarette lost to our own thoughts

And we take in our last drop of water-whiskey

A mirror reflecting back upon the other

Ain't no words needed after midnight

Just two bodies asleep in a new day's light

On this bus

With a destination ticker that reads; "ANYWHERE!"

I AM GHOST

It's just another night out

A drink or two with the living dead in the New Year

Mouths moving in conversation

But I no longer hear what they are saying

And the tap flows

Beer after beer

And ashtrays trade owners

As the butts pile higher and higher

And from here at the end of the bar

I watch the ritual of temporary resurrection

The communion of lifeless hearts

Just this ghost amongst rotting flesh marionettes

A presence barely indistinguishable from the smoke of a hundred cigarettes

Maybe it's better this way

Maybe it's more entertaining this way

Maybe I get my kicks this way

Maybe they're just jealous

Cause I can fade away just as fast as I had appeared

One snap of my fingers

A new place

A new time

A new life

And the tap flows

Beer after beer after beer after beer

Until all that remains is the sound of a last coffin closing

Maybe it's just better this way

Maybe, it's just better this way.

A LAST MOMENT IN ZWEIBRÜCKEN

5 AM

The city falls quiet

A silence so deafening it screams

A loneliness so crippling the heart cannot beat

A suffocation so gripping the hangman's noose is more gentle

Below the bridge, the river flows ever onwards to the sea

Utterly indifferent to what lay above

A place where dreams lay as bones

I let fall the butt of my last cigarette.

Adjust my scarf and coat a little tighter before grinding it into the cobblestone

Fall is coming

I turn to leave

The sound of my footsteps echoing

Already a memory here to any

The most lonely place on earth, anywhere.

The Author

Brian Dennis Hartford is a published author and writer of fiction, romance, and poetry. He has a bachelor's degree in security management and has worked in the private security industry for over twenty years. He currently resides in Europe with his wife and a cat named Noodles Nosferatu.

A Special Thanks

To my wife, family, and friends who have made this all possible. To The Hobbit, a place dearest to my heart. To its owner, Peter, for taking in strays like me. To Carla, we share the same heart for things long past us now. To the unknown woman at the bar (cover photo) love is never too late, we share one of the most romantic moments I have ever had, though I suspect, you've already forgotten it. And last, to Zweibrücken the loneliest place I have ever lived, goodbye.

Cover Photo Source Credits

Photo: Brian Denis Hartford, The Hobbit, Zweibrücken, 2024.
Unknown woman.
Created with Affinity Photo 2.5

Special Notes

The poem "CARLA" is a prelude poem to a future novel entitled CARLA by Brian Dennis Hartford. All rights reserved.

www.ingramcontent.com/pod-product-compliance
Lightning Source LLC
Chambersburg PA
CBHW032133090426
42743CB00007B/579